D0517333

NOV 2 5 2000

The Most Significant Archeological Find in the 20th Century

Terra Cotta Warriors

PEOPLE'S CHINA PUBLISHING HOUSE
BEIJING   CHINA

ISBN 7-80065-590-3
Published by
People's China Publishing House
No. 3 Chegongzhuang Road
Beijing, China
Zip: 100044

UNITED NATIONS EDUCATIONAL,
SCIENTIFIC AND
CULTURAL ORGANIZATION

CONVENTION CONCERNING
THE PROTECTION OF THE WORLD
CULTURAL AND NATURAL
HERITAGE

The World Heritage Committee
has inscribed

The Mausoleum of the First Qin Emperor

on the World Heritage List

Inscription on this List confirms the exceptional
and universal value of a cultural or
natural site which requires protection for the benefit
of all humanity

DATE OF INSCRIPTION
11 December 1987

DIRECTOR-GENERAL
OF UNESCO

UNESCO has listed the Qin Mausoleum as a world cultural heritage.

Preface

YUAN ZHONGYI

The burial site of the Qin terra cotta warriors and horses was discovered 1.5 kilometers east of the Qin Shi Huang Mausoleum, Lintong County, Shaanxi Province. The sacrificial objects honoring Qin Shi Huang, China's first emperor, were buried in three separate trenches which archeologists delineated as No. 1 Trench, No. 2 Trench and No. 3 Trench.

The initial discovery came in 1974 when local farmers digging a well unearthed broken pieces of Terra cotta soldiers. Archeologists discovered trenches No. 1 and No. 2 a short two years later. The three trenches, which cover a total of slightly over 20,000 square meters, hold a large number and variety of invaluable relics, including the 30 wooden war chariots, more than 2,000 life-size terra cotta warriors and horses, and more than 30,000 bronze weapons thus far verified. However, based on existing discoveries, archeologists estimate that the burial site will eventually yield more than 100 war chariots, 600 terra cotta horses and more than 7,000 terra cotta soldiers, as well as a large cache of bronze weapons.

The battle array of the terra cotta soldiers and horses serve as a reminder of the powerful forces of the Qin State. For example, the rectangular battle array of infantrymen and war chariots in No. 1 Trench includes some 6,000 warriors and horses, while the semi-circular array in No. 2 Trench consists of over 1,300 soldiers and horses, and No. 3 Trench yielding a war chariot, four horses and 68 warriors. The arrangement in the first two trenches suggests the battle arrays were positioned to guard the command post found in the third trench.

The various postures and vivid facial expressions reveal the quite different personalities of the terra cotta figurines. The artistic charm of the bold and concise style of sculpturing is readily discernible, with art experts noting that the terra cotta figurines reveal the outstanding artistic attainments of highly skilled Qin Dynasty craftsmen who had developed their own unique style. The Qin terra cotta figurines, which not only protected the nation's heritage but also opened the door to the future, are of epoch-making significance in the history of Chinese sculpture.

The discovery of the burial site of terra cotta figurines representing the Qin Dynasty army immediately created a sensation worldwide. The Qin terra cotta warriors and horses, a great marvel in the history of ancient civilization, were honored as "the eighth wonder of the world," and "the most significant archeological discovery in the Twentieth Century. " In December 1987, UNESCO listed the Qin Shi Huang Mausoleum, which includes the burial site of the terra cotta figures of the Qin army, as one of the world's cultural legacies.

Contents

I. Qin Shi Huang and His Burial Grounds

1. Qin Shi Huang, Emperor Through The Ages

Portrait of Emperor Qin Shi Huang.

Emperor Qin Shi Huang had the greatest and longest-lasting influence of over 300 emperors who ruled dynasties throughout Chinese history. He established China's first feudal empire, with the title "Huang Di" he created for feudal rulers reigning supreme throughout over 2,000 years feudal society.

Qin Shi Huang (259-210 B. C.), the First Emperor of the Qin Dynasty, was named Ying Zheng. The emperor, born in 259 B. C., had a beleaguered and unstable childhood due to frequent wars between the seven states existing during the period. His father, Yi Ren, son of the King of Qin, was held hostage in the State of Zhao. Thereafter, the family led a miserable life until Lu Buwei, a wealthy merchant doing business in Zhao, exhibited great political foresight when recognizing that Yi Ren was an important figure. Lu not only presented his favorite concubine to Yi, but also spent a great deal of money helping him return to his home state. Lu's generosity enabled Yi Ren to finally fulfill his long-held wish of ascending to the Qin throne.

Ying Zheng became the King of Qin at a tender age of 13 following the death of his father. Ying Zheng was much too young to administer state affairs and power quite naturally fell into the hands of Lu Buwei, who served as prime minister, and the empress dowager. In 238 B. C., Ying Zheng, 22, assumed control of state affairs and immediately erased the power of both the Empress Dowager as represented by Lao Ai, and that of Lu Buwei. He then set about fulfilling his ambition to create a powerful state by appointing Li Si as prime minister and selecting talented and capable men to strengthen his cabinet.

Ying Zheng soon adopted Li Si's advice and prepared for war to gain control of the other six states and unite the country. Qin troops overran the State of Han in 236 B. C. and then proceeded to defeat the Zhao, Wei, Chu, Yan and Qi states. In 221 B. C., Ying Zheng established the first centralized feudal monarchy in Chinese history.

Ying Zheng considered his success in unifying the country as a great contribution which far surpassed the accomplishments of "San Huang" and "Wu Di", rulers in remote antiquity. He then used the given names of his two predecessors to coin the title "Huang Di" (Emperor) to signify his supreme sacred status as a feudal ruler. Ying Zheng founded a feudal monarchy and became emperor with the name "Shi Huang. " While Qin Shi Huang boasted that his dynasty would last forever, it quite unexpectedly lasted for only two reigns. The dynasty, in fact, collapsed only four years after his death in 210 B. C. Nonetheless, the title "Emperor" he created lasted for more than 2,000 years throughout feudal society.

Qin Shi Huang attempted to effectively administer the

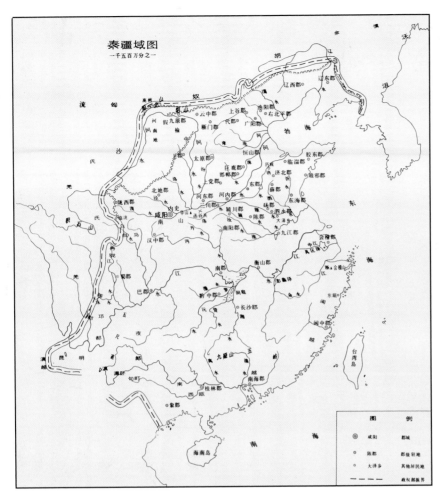

The State of Qin　(map).

country by introducing political, economic and cultural reform based on unification. He once again accepted Li Si's advice and abolished the enfeoffment system based on a system of prefectures and counties. Qin Shi Huang retained a firm grip on both military and administrative powers. He insisted that "everything should be settled according to law" and indeed used law as an important means of managing the country. His introduction of unified Chinese characters, currency and meteorology not only benefited economic development and cultural exchanges, but have had a strong and lasting influence on China.

Qin Shi Huang ordered the construction of a road system linking the former Yan, Qi, Wu and Chu areas, as well as number of roads especially for imperial use. The system eventually formed played an extremely important role in ancient transportation and economic exchanges. The emperor also confiscated weapons from the citizenry and implemented a system under which five households or 10 individuals were subject to punishment if one member of said groups committed an offence. The emperor also moved 120,000 wealthy families from across the country to develop the city of Xianyang, and sent merchants, slaves and criminals to develop border and remote areas. The policy he introduced exerted great influence on the history of China.

Qin Shi Huang quite obviously made great contributions which overshadowed those of his predecessors. The emperor firmly believed he possessed deifying powers. He visited Mt. Tai to offers a grand sacrifice to the Heavens, visited famous mountains on several occasions and built China's 10-thousand li Great Wall and hundreds of imperial palaces, including the well-known E'Pang Palace.

The emperor's confidence level declined somewhat at the prospect of death, and he commissioned the construction of his tomb while still a young man. Nonetheless, he sought ways to live a long life. For example, he once sent several thousands male and female teenagers on sea voyage in search of immortals. Regardless of the efforts, the emperor failed to attain immortality. Qin Shi Huang, 50, died from a sudden illness in 210 B. C. while visiting Shaqiu Pingtai (the northwest part of today's Guangzong, Hebei Province). His death sparked uprisings across the country and the Qin Dynasty came to an end in 206 B. C.

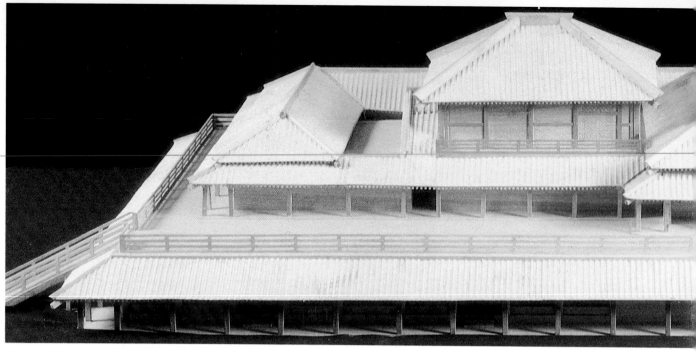

Model of the Qin Xian'yang Palace.

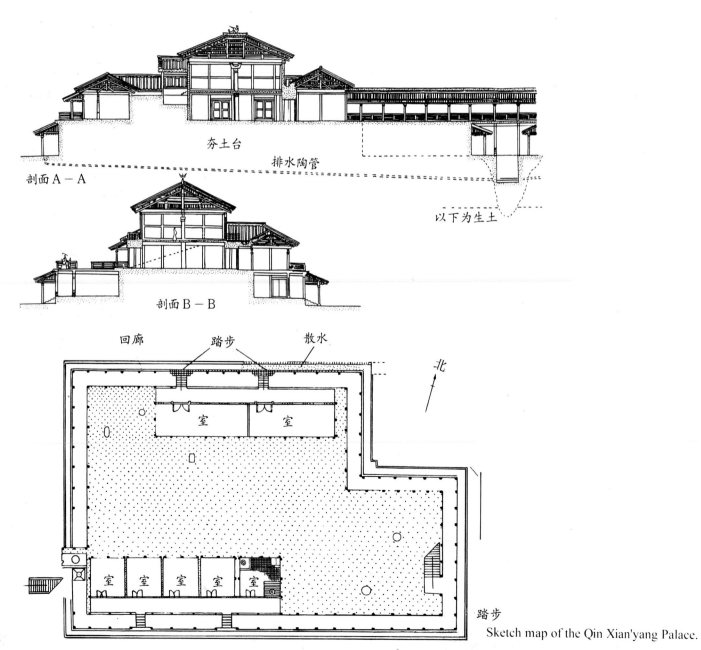

夯土台

排水陶管

剖面A－A

以下为生土

剖面B－B

回廊　　　踏步　　　散水

北

室　　室

室　室　室　室　室

踏步

Sketch map of the Qin Xian'yang Palace.

The tragic fall of Qin was the direct result of Qin Shi Huang's brutal rule. He attempted to strengthen his rule by introducing severe penal codes, extorting excessive taxes and levies, and burdening people with endless demands in total disregard of their already severe hardships. Nearly one-tenth of the population was involved in successive years of wars, or otherwise building the Great Wall, roads and famous buildings. Qin Shi Huang not only created countless disaster adversely affecting the people, but also devastated the development of productive social forces.

Qin Shi Huang attempted to wipe out heresy by burning almost all classic works, excluding books on medicine, divination and agriculture. He also ordered that over 460 Confucianists be buried alive. Those who dared disregard the law or express their opinions on state affairs would be killed along with their entire families. The emperor's actions thus brought untold calamity to the nation.

Nonetheless, the Qin Dynasty exhibited greatness in some areas and indeed added brilliance to Chinese history. Changes and reforms to systems and traditions introduced during the period affected the entire feudal society. The contemporary world continues to refer to China as Qin, or as Chin according to the original transliteration. Neighboring countries greatly admired the brilliant material civilization and technical achievements of the Qin Dynasty. The Qin developed high standards for agriculture, craftsmanship, bronze casting, silk and weaving.

The astonishing difference between creativity and destruction during the Qin made Qin Shi Huang a controversial leader, with contradictions ranging from a brutal tyrant to a peculiar but great leader, and the eternal emperor.

Few historical documents cover the long history of Qin, and one can only appreciate the period's brilliant material civilization through cultural relics. Qin cultural relics are a source of amazement from the standpoint of the imperial culture. People are indeed amazed at the 10-thousand li Great Wall, the awesomenesses and magnificence of the Xianyang, E'Pang and Jieshi palace ruins. The amazement and appreciation not only extends to the then several hundred palaces built in the areas radiating hundreds of miles from Xianyang, but also to the frescoes, sculptures, cast art work, craftsmanship and agricultural proficiency of the Qin. The Qin Mausoleum represents an era of cruelty and misery, as well as creativity and brilliance.

Qin Shi Huang, a brutal but great historical figure, left the immense and monumental Qin Mausoleum, a creation mixed with both blood and tears.

The Qin Mausoleum.

2. Qin Shi Huang Burial Grounds

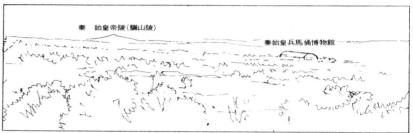

The Qin Mausoleum and the Museum of Terra Cotta Warriors and Horses.

The Qin Mausoleum, located in Lintong County, Xi'an, Shaanxi Province, is surrounded by the Lishan Mountains to the south and the Weihe River to the north. Five peaks in the Lishan Mountains served as a backdrop for the rarely seen "lotus tomb" which coincides traditional Chinese geomantic omens. The site, surrounded by mountains and rivers, was an ideal burial site for feudal emperors who believed they would lead a new life in another world.

Construction of the Qin Mausoleum, the largest imperial tomb in China, began in 247 B. C. soon after Qin Shi Huang ascended to the throne and was still underway at his death 210 B. C. Construction of auxiliary projects was halted in 208 B. C. when troops surrounded the imperial capital during an uprising.

Numerous groups of people worked on the 39-years construction project, from high-ranking officials such as Prime Minister Li Si who was in charge of the work, to criminals forced to do manual labor. As many as 720,000 workers from across the country helped construct the tomb.

Criminals were forced to cut and transport massive logs from a thousand miles away, as well as large stones from hundreds of miles distant. Numerous laborers died from hard labor carried out for many years. The unmatched immense magnificent mausoleum represents a solemn, but nonetheless stirring segment in the history of China.

The mausoleum, which covers 56.25 square km. was designed in accordance with the layout of the emperor's capital. The original tomb, measuring some 115 meters in height, was covered with dirt. The remaining 76 meters of the structure resemble a topless pyramid. A city wall, measuring four meters in height and four meters in width, encircles the buried palace. The wall, constructed of unfired bricks, has gates on four sides.

The tomb was originally surrounded by two rectangular walls some eight meters thick, with the outer wall stretching 6,264 meters and the inner 3,870 meters. Both walls featured corner towers and broad gates on four sides, with the arrangement resembling a real city. Pieces of tile, gate stones and piles of red soil are all that remain of the once magnificent structure. High walls, measuring one meter in height, can be found in Yuejiagou and Xiachen villages located at the southern end of the tomb complex. The sections allow one the southern end of the tomb complex. The sections allow one to clearly see the denseness of layers which are between five and seven centimeters thick. The thick flat loam walls, which are strong as bricks, represent the wonderful craftsmanship found thousands of years ago.

Hundreds of auxiliary tombs, both large and small, have been found inside and outside the walls of the cemetery, including 10 sacrificial trenches, with the complex symbolizing the overall layout of the capital. Ongoing archeological work continues to yield more traces of structures and artifacts, including the imperial burial palace, side palaces, gardens and temples. The excavated sites include the bronze cart and horse trench, the western tomb construction site, horse trench, rare bird and animal trench, tombs for the princes and princesses of Shangjiao Village and tomb builders from Zhaobeihu Village. Each of the sites has enriched our knowledge and understanding of the Qin system, culture, clothing and material civilization. The discoveries have not only peaked our curiosity, but also offer bright prospects for archeological work.

(1) Remains of the Mausoleum

The mausoleum was once a brilliant architectural complex with numerous buildings. Archeologists working over sev-

Yuefu Bell: This finely crafted 13cm bell was excavated from a hall in the western part of the Qin Mausoleum in 1976.

eral decades have discovered and excavated several dozen construction sites covering tens of thousands of square meters, including the most important large tomb, gardens, temples and houses.

The square ruins of the imperial burial palace cover 3,575 square meters on the north side of the tomb. The structure has a finely crafted pedestal foundation, and is thought to have been constructed with a hipped-roof encircled by single winding corridors. Broken pieces of tile and red clay are scattered across the area, with interior sections of white-washed walls coated with mixture of earth and wheat grass. The bases of stone columns and neatly arranged apron are still easily distinguishable around the site. The imperial burial palace, which appears to have been based on the pre-Qin tomb style, was built as an integral component close to the main tomb, instead of inside it. This particular approach represented the introduction of a new system for constructing mausoleums.

A group of six buildings stretching east to west are found some 50 meters north of the imperial burial palace. The large site, which covers 4,800 square meters, is 240 meters long from east to west and 20 meters wide. Most of the hipped-roof or quadrangular buildings face north, with a small group facing west. The 50 meter long flagstone apron, 55cm square plinth stones, drainage ditch, finely crafted stone water drainage system and red interior walls show the architectural skill and magnificence of the construction itself.

Large foundations are found on a site with four buildings laid out east to west which is located further to the north. The solid smooth floors, blue flat stones inlaid in the walls, stone steps, ridge ornaments shaped like and owl's tail, eaves tiles and knocker base are all extremely attractive. The exquisitely crafted corrosive-proof tiles, with a diameter of 61cm amazing, are decorated with vivid patterns and were designed to

protect the tenons. The highly artistic architecture enables one to easily imagine the former grandeur of the ancient mausoleum.

Gardens, temples and houses have been found in three separate locations in the western section of the complex, both inside and outside the walls. Large numbers of cloud-shaped tiles and other building materials have also been unearthed, along with dozen of objects such a bronze bell inlaid with gold and silver. The bell, carved with "Yue Fu", is a rare treasure indeed. It provides ample proof that the Qin established a "Yue Fu" office responsible for collecting folk songs and ballads to entertain the imperial court. It also indicates the colorful life of the period existing in spite of the stifling environment prevailing under the dictatorship of feudal rulers.

(2) Sacrificial Trenches

A group of sacrificial cart and horse trenches covering 3,025 square meters were unearthed some 20 meters west of the Qin Mausoleum. One trench, measuring seven meters in length and 2.3 meters in width, was excavated in 1980 and yielded two large colored and decorated bronze carts and horses. The combination of carts and horses reveal the high-level skill of Chinese forefathers and show the complicated style of carts, casting and sculpturing and processing techniques characteristic of the period.

The large number of horses buried with the dead is indicative of the importance the animals played in daily life. Sacrificial horse trenches have been unearthed in two locations, one in the eastern part of the outer tomb wall, and the other between the inner and outer walls. Their location indicates that Qin Shi Huang had stables both inside and outside the capital city.

Ninety-nine horse trenches, most of which hold one horse, have been excavated in the outer sacrificial stable. The horses

A section of underground pottery drainage system which is 60cm in height and 50cm in width.

A Qin brick.

are closely arranged in three line formations running from the south to the north. Despite the fact that only skeletal remains exist, a knife found in the mouth of one horse indicates that horses were killed prior to burial. Many painted figurines of kneeling horsemen have also been found. The vivid masterpieces of art are still in good condition. Various unearthed objects bear inscriptions such as "middle stable", "palace stable", "left stable" and "small stable". Similar names found in the "Jiuyuan Lu" (imperial stables) section of the "Written Bamboo Slips of Qin Mausoleum" clearly show the functions of the stables.

The stables feature quite different layouts, with the inner stable found in the large L-shaped trench featuring wood stalls. Each stall holds an orderly array of three horses. Several hundred horses were unearthed in the trenches along with a number of figurines of horsemanship instructors standing behierarchy is readily discernible when compared the previously mentioned figurines with those of other horsemen measuring 70cm in height.

Sacrificial trenches of rare birds and animals were discovered in the western section between the outer and inner walls. The 31 trenches are arranged in three lines running from the south to the north. Each trench in the middle line holds an earthen coffin filled with bones, with animals buried separately according to their species. Metal rigs found around the necks of some horses indicate that they were once tied in their stables. All trenches in the outer two lines yielded a kneeling figurine measuring between 68-73cm in height. The figurines most likely represent stablemen.

The largest and most attractive sacrificial trench is without a doubt the one holding the Qin terra cotta army. Three trenches, which cover over 20,000 square meters, hold well over 7,000 life-size terra cotta horses and armoured warriors.

More than 1,000 pottery figurines and real weapons have been discovered in the small one-sixth section of the No. 1 Trench thus far excavated. The monumental discovery has indeed caught the attention of hundreds of thousands people from throughout the world.

(3) Auxiliary Tombs Reveal Obsession With Hierarchy

Auxiliary tombs are found in four sections of the Qin Mausoleum: the northern section in the city itself features 28 small to medium size auxiliary; with other tombs found in the western section between the city walls, and the outer eastern and western sections.

The largest auxiliary tomb is found in the western section of the city. The inner area of the tomb measures 15.5 meters in length and 14.5 meters in width, and is fronted by an entry pathway stretching 15.8 meters. A red coat of paint and ashes have been discovered in the tomb. The position and standard characteristics of the structure tells that the owner should be Prince Gao, Qin Shi Huang's son who chose death rather than the throne and requested "to be buried at the foot of Lishan Mountain near his father". Second emperor Hu Hai gave Gao 100,000 coins for funeral expenses.

A mysterious group of 48 auxiliary tombs have been found in the western section between the inner and outer walls. The fact than nothing has been found in the tombs adds even greater mystery to the burial site.

Auxiliary tombs found in Shangjiao Village to the east of the outer wall have also attracted great attention. The 17 tombs are neatly arranged in a single line stretching from the south to the north. Eight tombs excavated in 1976 yielded 200 pieces gold and silver, as well as a number of sacrificial objects made of bronze and iron. Various objects were inscribed with the words "Shao Fu" (Young Master's Mansion)

A standard weight of the Qin.

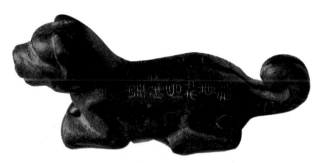

This tiger-shaped tally inlaid with gold measures 3.4cm in height and 8.9cm in length. Qin Shi Huang issued the tally to instruct his generals concerning appropriate troop deployments.

or with "Rong Lu" (Honor and Fortune), with other objects including personal stamps and letters. The objects indicate that the tombs held the remains of members of the royal family. The scene offers evidence that the victims, between 23-30 years of age, were murdered, with the mutilated bodies of some chopped into several pieces, and still others having been shot or hanged.

One history book points to the fact that the auxiliary tombs hold the remains of princes and princesses killed by Hu Hai after he usurped power and the throne. Hu Hai was afraid the brothers and sisters would imperil his power and thus ordered their death. He then granted them the honor of "accompanying their father".

Two auxiliary tomb sites are thought to have existed three miles southwest of the Qin Mausoleum. However, the tomb once located north of Yaochitou Village was apparently damaged beyond recognition and has not as yet been located. The second tomb to the west of Zhaobeihu Village covers 8,100 square meters, with the overall layout measuring 180 meters in length from the south to the north and 45 meters in width.

The 103 tombs in burial site #32 were excavated in 1978. The tombs held the skeletal remains of 100 people, but failed to yield coffins or other objects. A single tomb, however, did hold one simple tile coffin. Inscriptions found on tile pieces recorded the native homes, names, positions and job titles of 19 entombed people. The inscriptions indicate the people from six conquered states were sentenced to hard labor because of the inability to pay various types of fines. The pieces represent the earliest tomb inscriptions found in China.

(4) Mysterious Underground Palace

"Records of the Historian: Biographic Sketches of Qin Shi Huang", the earliest and most dependable record, states: "

Qin Shi Huang gained power and shortly thereafter began building his tomb on Lishan Mountain. More than 700,000 people from across the country participated in the construction project. The dug deep into the earth, fashioned outer coffins with melted copper and buried money, valuables and treasures, as well as rare birds and animals. Crossbows were installed to kill anyone attempting to rob the tomb. Mercury was used to symbolize surging rivers, lakes and the sea. The tomb held everything in the world, including objects related to astronomy and geography. Lamps were filled with 'renyu' cream to ensure an eternal flame".

Sima Qian, author of the aforementioned work, provided a detailed depiction of the miraculous tomb.

Archeologists and experts from many other disciplines have worked together to explore the secrets of Qin Shi Huang's underground palace. Between 1981-1982, Chang Yong and Li Tong worked under the leadership of professors Xie Xuejin and Zheng Kangle and in close cooperation with the archeological team to test the mercury content in the center section of the sealed Qin Mausoleum. They found that a 12,000 square-meter area contained an unusually strong mercury content. The variations of travelling mercury was 70-1500PPb, a level more than 10 times that of dirt in surrounding areas. The differing levels quite obviously resulted from the volatilization and infiltration of mercury buried in rounding areas. The differing levels quite obviously resulted from the volatilization and infiltration of mercury buried in the tomb, and thus proved the accuracy of Sima Qian's descriptions.

The use of such a large quantity of mercury to symbolize rivers, lakes and the sea to differentiate between the human and nether worlds quite obviously symbolize that the emperor would always rule the land. Ancient people referred to

The vivid facial expression of this some 70cm tall kneeling figurine is of the standard design fashioned by a combination sculpturing and painting.

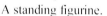

A standing figurine.

water as a symbol of longitude and when building the tomb applied the concept to create geographical features such as mountains and rivers for the dead. To some extent, at least, this not only reflected the development of geographical science in ancient China, but also the characteristic design of the Qin Mausoleum which pursued the unique and involved bold creative imaginations. Ancient people pursued the imperial eternity and attempted to perfect the imaginary in terms of reality. They indeed wanted the rivers and sea to flow for eternity. The design established an unequalled record which will never again be matched. The feat also reveals the Qin achievement in the development and use of mercury.

Astronomical features in the buried palace are reflected in paintings. "Studies of Terra Cotta Soldiers and Horses of the Qin Dynasty", written by Shaanxi Archeologist Yuan Zhongyi, describes the astronomical paintings in the tomb thusly: "A golden toad symbolizing the sun, a jade hare the moon and other stars in a round red design. " Astronomical paintings of this kind were first found in the Zenghouyi Tomb, a tomb dating to the early Warring States Period (475-221 B. C.), in Suixian County, Hubei Province. Similar works were later found in various Western Han Tombs (206 B. C. -24 A. D. in Luoyang, Henan Province, and were, in fact, recently unearthed from another Western Han Tomb on the campus of Xi'an Communications University in Shaanxi Province. The discoveries have readily proved Yuan's conjecture.

The work "Hundreds Imperial Palaces" describes buried palaces as models of imperial palaces. Qin Shi Huang spent his lifetime abusing available manpower to build numerous pavilions and villas for his travels. The E'Pang Palace was still under construction at his death, and models of various structures were buried in his tomb.

What are the actual dimensions of tombs with such a rich content?

"Records of the Historian" and "The Han Book" point out that underground palaces were usually built at a depth reaching or slightly below the third layer of groundwater. In 1982, the Qin Mausoleum Archeological Team cleared a Qin well located in the northwestern section between the inner and outer walls and measured the existing water level at 16 meters deep. The discovery led to the inference that the underground palace was constructed at a depth of 20 meters or more. In fact, the tomb of one Qin duke, whose social status would have in no way compared with that of Qin Shi Huang, was constructed at a depth of 25 meters. "The Old Han Rites" stipulates that a Han emperor's tomb should be constructed at a depth of 30 meters and should cover 6.6666 hactares. The depth of the Qin Mausoleum, a structure which is much larger than a Han tomb, has thus been estimated at over 30 meters.

The first problem when constructing a deep underground palace centered on preventing groundwater seepage. The classic work entitled "The Han Book, the Biography of Jia Shan" records the following clue to the process: "Line the walls with stones, solidify the interior wall with melted copper, and coat the outer wall with red lacquer. " A further clarification in "The Han Book" reads: "Prevent groundwater seepage be using stones and painting the exterior wall with lacquer. "

Construction of the tomb required a large quantity of stones. Various historical documents concerning construction of the tomb note that hundreds of thousands of criminals were forced to carry stones from the North Mountains. The stone processing site in Zhengjia Village shows that at least 750,000 square meters of stones were used to construct the

A deer pattern
eaves tile.

This half-round eaves tile,
measuring 48cm in height and 61cm in diameter,
represents the largest ancient tiles thus discovered
in China. The tile was unearthed in the northern
ruins of the burial grounds in 1977.

Qin Mausoleum.

Stones used for the mausoleum were carved with beautiful patterns and painted with moisture-proof red lacquer. Seams between the stones was filled with melted copper and tin. An even more complicated, and as yet undetermined, method was undoubtedly used to cover the mouths of springs. One hint to the process can be found at the tomb of Empress Wu Ze Tian of the Tang Dynasty (618-907). Seams between stones were filled with melted iron to prevent groundwater from seeping into the tomb.

Various surveys have indicated that the top of the Qin underground palace measures 460 meters in length from the south to the north and 392 meters in width. Based on architectural principles and comparing degradation slopes in other large tombs indicates that the floor of the palace rests at a depth of 50 meters, with the edges of the rectanglar stretching about 250 meters each. The area of the groundwater surface is thought to be much larger, with estimates of the edges reaching as high as 320 meters. According to said estimates, the area under the groundwater level covers at least 300,000 square meters, and was constructed using stones and seams filled with melted copper. Constructing such a grand and complicated project would be difficult to achieve even today.

The primary focus of the extensive construction efforts, including the use of mercury and secret crossbows, was to prevent intrusions by graverobbers. The practice of robbing tombs was simply an auxiliary result of elaborate funeral customs. Graverobbers, which appeared as early as the Warring States Period, were a major concern of both the imperial and wealthy families.

Designers racked their brains to ensure the security of the Qin Mausoleum, the most luxurious tomb in China, with history proving their success. Not a single sign has yet been found indicating that the security of the tomb has been breached. Archeological surveys verify the integrity of all walls and gates, as well as earthen seal covering the tomb. However, several holes reaching a depth of some 10 meters indicate attempts by would-be graverobbers. Successfully robbing the secure tomb would have indeed required a herculean effort. Archeologists are quite obviously delighted that the treasures of the Qin Mausoleum have remained safely in the nether world awaiting excavation.

(5) Other Ruins

Many other tombs, unrelated to the Qin Mausoleum, have been found in the area, including ruins at the Five-Ranges Dam, the Zhengjia Village Stone Processing Site and the Fish-pond Site. Intensified archeological work is expected to yield even more fascinating discoveries.

II. Trenches Yielding Sacrificial Figurines of Terra Cotta Soldiers and Horses

1. Monumental Discovery:

Pottery figurines unearthed in the No. 1 Trench.

Yang Zhifa and two other farmers in Xiyang, a small indescribable village in eastern Lintong County, Shaanxi Province, found broken pieces of pottery figurines and bronze arrowheads while digging a well on a chilly early spring morning in March 1974. Their find led to the excavation of yet another wonder of the world. The news, which spread quickly to Xi'an and then Beijing, astonished the world.

Archeological team of Shaanxi archaeologists, including Yuan Zhongyi, arrived the tomb site in May 1974 and launched the most important excavation project of the century.

The well the farmers were digging was later determined to located at the southeast corner of the No. 1 Trench. The farmers reached a depth of two meters and encountered a layer of firm red earth. They continued digging and found broken pieces of pottery figurines, bronze arrowheads and bricks. The surprised farmers failed to realize the significance of their discovery. Yang Zhifa filled his cap with arrowheads, and later sold to the Sanren Purchasing and Marketing Agency for only two yuan per half kilo. The digging team nonchalantly tossed the pieces of pottery into a nearby field. Some villagers began collecting bricks which were supposedly beneficial to one's health if placed in pillowcase.

Fang Shumiao, the cadre in charge of water conservancy in the township, visited Xiyang Village and found the discarded Qin pottery pieces and bronze arrowheads. Fang was uncertain whether or not the object were relics, but nonetheless suggested: "Why not send them to the county cultural center.

Actual relics are worth money. "

The farmers loaded two carts with pottery pieces and journeyed eight kilometers to the county cultural center. The seemingly insignificant 10 yuan they received for the objects was in fact a virtual bonanza for farmers in the 1970s.

The inadvertent find of the farmers did not, in fact, represent the very first exploration of the tomb area. Archeologists excavating the No. 1 and No. 2 trenches had previously found more than 20 tombs, both large or small, dating as far back as the Han Dynasty. The area was also dotted with two wells and several holes dug by would-be graverobbers.

A few years earlier, farmers digging in the area of the No. 1 Trench uncovered the heads of two figurines at the north end of a seven-meter deep ditch. The farmers were at a loss when trying to decide what to do with their unexpected find. They eventually decided to return to the village and seek the advice of elders. No decision was reached to group sought the advice of Yang Tianfa's 85-year-old mother, the oldest villager. She had no recollection of a temple ever having been located near the village. The farmers failed to find any traces of the figurines, and thereafter dared not touch the heads. Time passed and the two heads disappeared, with nothing but ashes and unburned pieces of paper found where they had been stored. It turned out that a soft-hearted elderly woman had buried the heads in another location.

Archeologists were prepared for the arrival of the next opportunity. Zhao Kangmin, director of the county cultural

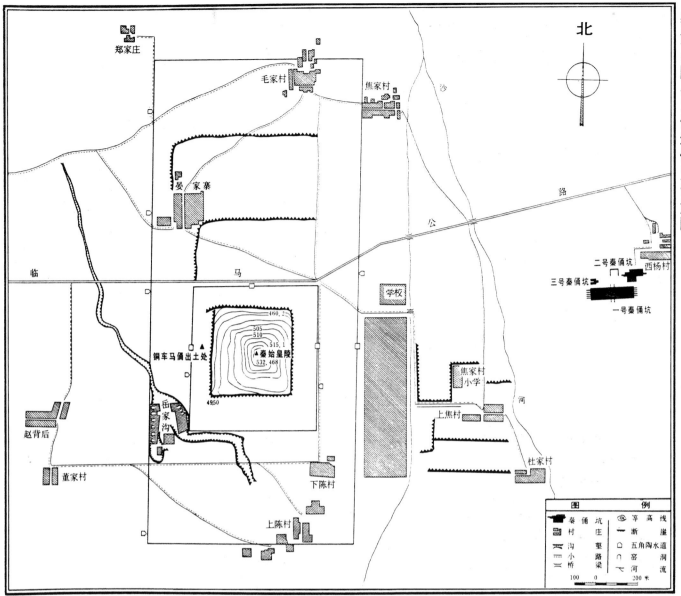

北

郑家庄

毛家村

焦家村

沙

路

公

晏　家寨

临

马

铜车马俑出土处

460.2
505
510
515.1
▲秦始皇陵
532.468

岳家沟

赵背后

董家村

下陈村

上陈村

二号秦俑坑　西杨村

三号秦俑坑

一号秦俑坑

学校

焦家村小学

上焦村

河

杜家村

图	例	
秦俑坑	等高线	
村庄	断崖	
沟壑	五角陶水道	
小路	窑洞	
桥梁	河流	

100　0　　　　200 米

Sketch map of sacrificial trenches.

Yang Zhifa, one of the farmers who first found the Qin figurines.

17

The first terra cotta figurines and architectural ruins
were unearthed at the east end of the No. 1 Trench.

Excavated corner of the No. 1 Trench.

Excavation of the No. 1 Trench.

Excavated section at the rear of the No. 1 Trench.

center, brimmed with excitement when Yang Zhifa arrived at the center with more pieces of pottery figurines. Zhao immediately went to Xiyang Village to conduct an on-the-spot investigation. He proceeded to confiscate the arrowheads from the purchasing and marketing agency and recovered more than 40 Qin bricks from villagers.

Shortly thereafter the archeological team began excavating the front section of the No. 1 Trench, and simultaneously conducted an extensive survey of the surrounding area. They named the trenches according to the order in which they were excavated. The excitement grew as work continued. They initially planned to complete their work within a few months, but soon determined that several decades would be required to complete the project. They soon knew that important discoveries could be made at anytime, and that untold wonders and historical treasure troves were buried beneath their feet.

The No. 2 Trench was discovered in May, 1976, as the team explored the northern section at the east end of the No.

Excavated corner of the No. 1 Trench.

Preparatory to an excavation of the eastern side of the No. 1 Trench.

1 Trench. The No. 3 Trench was found in July while the team was working in the northern section just to the west of the No. 1 Trench. The discoveries proved the area of the large-scale sacrificial trenches holding figurines of terra cotta soldiers and horses in the Qin Mausoleum covered over 20,000 square meters. The mausoleum, in fact, housed more than 7,000 life-size terra cotta horses and armoured warriors, more than 100 wooden war chariots and many exquisite ancient weapons. People worldwide referred to the discovery as a large-scale "buried military camp" and "ancient art museum". The discovery was, in fact, the world's most important archeological achievement in this century, with the site winning the title as the "eighth wonder of the world".

The auxiliary tomb of princes and princesses in Shangjiao Village was discovered in October 1976; the Qin imperial burial palace and side palaces were found in March 1977; the sacrificial trenches for rare birds and animals was unearthed in July 1977; the Zhaobeihu tomb holding the remains of construction workers and the trench of palace stables were discovered and excavated in 1979 and 1980 respectively. The sacrificial bronze carts and horses discovered in 1980 created yet another stir throughout the world.

Broken pieces of painted potteries
excavated from the No. 3 Trench.

The excavation site of the No. 3 Trench.

Archeologists at work.

Restoration and maintenance of unearthed figurines.

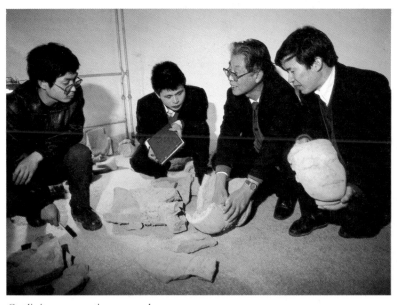
Outlining restoration procedures.

Restoring the head of figurines.

Delicate restoration effort.

Back of terra cotta figurines awaiting restoration.

Broken pieces from the heads of figurines.

Excavation of armorless infantry in the No. 1 Trench.

Terra cotta horses unearthed on the No. 1 Trench.

Excavated section at the rear of the No. 1 Trench.

Rear view of the battle array in the No. 1 Trench. Most terra cotta figurines in the section have not been restored.

2. Architectural Structure:

Patterns found in dirt covering the trenches
proved that straw mats were used to cave-ins.

The sacrificial trench holding the figurines of soldiers and horses is located 1.5 kilometers east of the Qin Mausoleum. The design of the underground architectural complex was based on a military camp. The three camps vary in size, with one camp fronting two rear camps which stand side by side. The camps are found in the No. 1, No. 2 and No. 3 trenches.

The following steps were required to construct the basically wood and earthen structures:

The first step involved digging a large rectangular trench with a solid foundation;

Second, the trenches were lined with loam walls running from the east to the west. The functions of the wall were to either separate space or bear the weight of the roof;

Third, troughs dug on both the south and north sides of the separating walls and the four sides of the trench itself were supported with logs placed every 1.4-1.76 meters and additional logs to support the purlins. The logs created a monolithic bearing frame;

Fourth, rafters were secured to the walls and purlins to form the roof;

Fifth, the roof was covered with reed mats topped by a layer of moisture-proof red clay. Ceiling reached a height of 3.2 meters, bricks were used to form the flat floor and walls covered with mixture of grass and dirt;

Next, gates added to each side of the trench were sealed with logs and pounded earth following the placement of sacrificial objects;

The final step involved covering the structure with a layer of dirt some two meters thick.

The rectangular No. 1 Trench, the largest of the three, measures 230 meters in length from east to west, and 62 meters in width. The depth of the trench fluctuates between 4.5 and 6.5 meters. The trench features 20 sloping entryways, with five found on each side. The entryways on the eastern and western side, thought to be the main entrances, are between 14-28 meters in length and 3.8-6.6 meters in width. Gates on the eastern and western sides are 3.45 meters wide, while those on southern and northern sides measure two meters in width. The interior corridor has nine passageways, each of which measures 180 meters in length and 3.5 meters in width. The corridors link the eastern and western sections, with passageways separated by thick walls some 2.4 meters in width.

The No. 2 Trench, which includes four units, covers 6,000 square meters in the shape of a carpenter's square. The first unit, surrounded by corridor with four passageways linking the eastern and western section, is the easternmost protrusion in the trench and was a camp for archers. The second unit, which served as the camp for coachmen, is found in the southern section of the trench. This particular section includes two long corridors leading from the south to the north, and an additional eight passageways leading from east to west. The central or third unit which served as the camp for infantrymen, has three passageways. The fourth, the cavalry camp, found on the northernmost end of the trench three passageways stretching from east to west. The units in the trench, the most complicated structure in the complex which clearly delineates the divisions between units, are linked by gates.

The No. 3 Trench, which faces east, appears to represent a recessed plan. A 14-meter long sloping gateway and gate lead to the eastern central hall which holds a cart and horse. Two corridors in the hall lead to halls on both the north and south sides. The rectangular northern hall runs from the east to the west, and the southern hall complex

The oldest brick wall thus far discovered in China was found in the southeast corner of the No. 1 Trench. The said wall measures 1.65 meters in height, 0.85 meter in width and 0.5 meter in thickness.

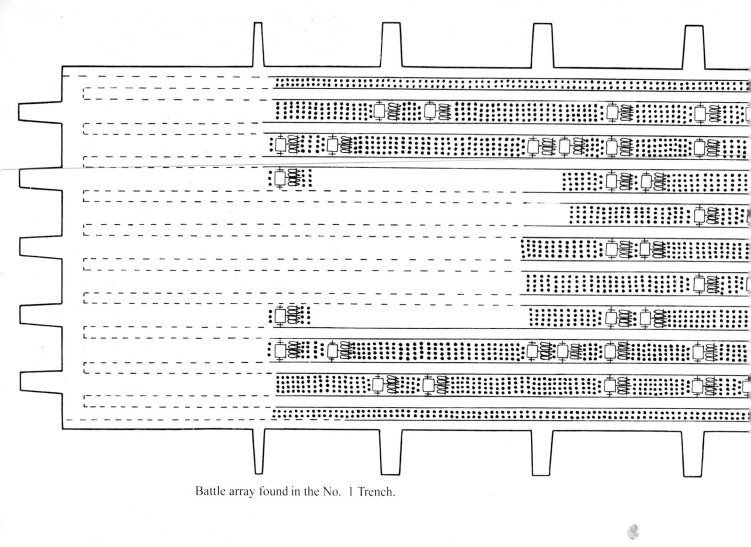

Battle array found in the No. 1 Trench.

Restored structures in the sacrificial trenches.

Sketch map of figurines lining up in the trenches.

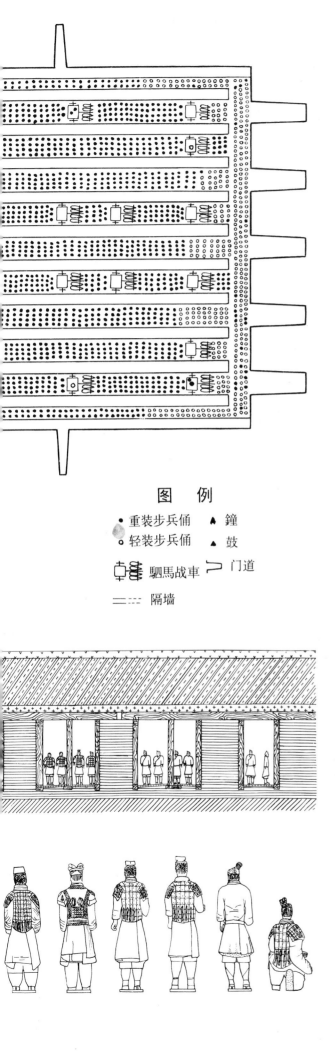

图 例

- 重装步兵俑 ▲ 鐘
○ 轻装步兵俑 ▲ 鼓

馹馬战車 ⌐ 门道

== ∷ 隔墙

Pathway leading to the south gate of the No. 1 Trench.

links the front and rear halls.

Qin Dynasty Strategist Wei Liao describes the camp layout in his "Wei Liao Zi". The actual architectural design of the buried sculptured legion perfectly matches Wei's description. Quite obviously, however, there is a world of difference between the actual palaces in which Qin Shi Huang lived and those found in the sacrificial trenches. Nonetheless, the detailed design, grand layout, complicated interior structure, fine construction materials and exquisite craftsmanship reflect the overall architectural level of the Qin Dynasty.

The fact that the No. 1 Trench and at least half of the No. 2 Trench were destroyed by fire represents a great loss. In addition, decay caused the collapse of the remaining part of the roof on the No. 2 trench, as well as the roof on the No. 3 Trench. An in-depth survey of the site proves that graverobbers sacked the trenches before they were burnt. Numerous pottery figurines were broken and untold number of weapons were removed soon after the complex was completed. According to the "Records of the Historian", Xiang Yu (232-202 B. C.), leader of the peasant uprising in 206 B. C. near the end of the Qin, led his army to destroy the Qin. His forces proceeded to burn numerous Qin palaces, including the Xianyang Palace, E'Pang Palace and the Qin Mausoleum. This has led some to surmise that the latter was one of the primary targets of the uprising.

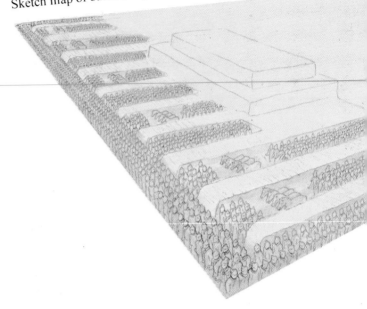

3. Powerful Buried Army:

The Qin army, the military power of the period, featured "thousands of carriages and chariots, tens of thousand of horses and hundreds of thousands of armoured men". The might of the army in fact enabled Qin Shi Huang made his contributions and establish his state. The terra cotta horses and armoured warriors found in the trenches fully display the power of Qin in miniature.

No. 1 Trench

The battle array in the No. 1 Trench is the focal point in terms of both area and number of warriors. The trench holds more than 6,000 terra cotta horses and armoured warriors, with the four arrays representing the vanguard, main body, flank and rear guards. The vanguard of 204 warriors stand in three lines at the front of the trench facing east. The main body, directly behind the vanguard, consists of 36 groups of carts and warriors standing at various intervals. The flank formation consists of two groups of warriors, one each on the north and south sides. The rear guard form three lines at the back of the trench.

Armless members of the vanguard force have no helmets, with their hair instead formed into tall buns and their legs protected by rattan. Crossbows in hands indicate their unique fighting skill.

Heavily armed warriors stand in formation directly behind the vanguard. The legs of the armoured warriors are wrapped tightly, and they are positioned according the weapons they carry, including spears, battle-axes, halberds and crossbows.

The battle array coincides with Military Strategist Sun Bin's description of the art of war. The battle array fully displays an army's power and endurance during battles. Such an army could destroy strong enemy positions and easily defeat their inveterate foe.

Soldiers in the right and left flank formations used crossbows to battle the enemy. However, their main task was to closely watch the deployment of enemy forces. The responsibility of rear guard was to prevent an enemy from behind.

Armoured warriors were armed with real bronze weapons. While many weapons were lost during wars fought at the end of the Qin Dynasty, a large number of buried weapons have survived, and tens of thousand ancient weapons having already been unearthed.

The positioning of the warriors makes it is easy to determine the weapons they used and indeed to understand the nature of the battle array. Crossbows were widely used during the period, with the combined arrangement of warriors using both light and heavy weapons, and the relatively centralized sections of the force indicating that battles were much more complicated than those in earlier times.

Fifty wooden chariots found were pulled by teams of four horses. The shafts on the chariots measure 3.7 to 3.96 meter in length, with the bodies measuring 1.2 meters in length and 1.4 meters in width. Each coach has a 40cm railing and rear door, and the 1.35 meter wheels have 30 spokes. The chariots were painted with lacquer and exquisitely decorated with patterns.

Each chariot, which held a three-man team, including the charioteer, was surrounded by a small battle unit of between 50-100 infantrymen. Various analyses indicate the chariots with round canopies carried army officers responsible for drums and large bells used in war. Most chariots found in the No. 1 Trench are thought to have been command carts carrying generals who sat in the left seat barking orders and

Exterior view of Exhibition Hall of the No. 1 Trench. Based on the Chinese government decision made in 1975, the main hall of the Museum of Terra Cotta Warriors and Horses, which covers 15,460 square meters, was constructed on the site of No. 1 Trench in the same year and the museum opened to public on October 1, 1979.

either beating drums or ringing bells to indicate whether their forces should charge or retreat. The uneven distribution of the chariots indicates the highly complicated nature of a real battle array.

Appropriate battle arrays were considered an extremely important aspect of warfare in ancient times. "Six Battle Rules", a famous book on warfare dating to the Warring States Period, states: "A cavalryman is no match for an infantryman in hand-to-hand combat, but the former is fully able to defeat eight of the latter when in array. "

The "square battle array" in the No. 1 Trench represents one of the 10 formations listed in "Strategist Sun Bin: The Art of War", a work which has enhanced contemporary knowledge of warfare in ancient times.

Section of the battle array in the No. 1 Trench.

The No. 1 Trench measures 230 meters in length from east to west and 62 meters in width. The depth of the trench fluctuates between 4.5 and 6.5 meters. Approximately 20 percent of the trench, which covers about 12,600 square meters, has been excavated, and some 1,046 life-size terra cotta warriors and horses have been restored. The array of vanguard forces supported by flank and rear guards truly exhibits the grandeur of the powerful ancient Qin army.

The remnants of wood used to support
the roof on the No. 1 Trench.

Battle array in the No.
1 Trench viewed from the right.

Sectional rear view of the battle array in the No. 1 Trench prior to restoration.

Frontal view of a section
of the battle array in the No. 1
Trench following restoration.

Unearthed heads of terra cotta horses from the No. 1 Trench.

Section of the battle array in the No. 1 Trench.

Infantrymen in the No. 1 Trench.

Section of the battle array in the No. 1 Trench.

39

▶ Battle array in the No. 1
Trench viewed from the rear.

Battle array in the No. 1
Trench viewed from the left.

Battle array in the No. 1 Trench viewed from the right.

Four horses hitch pulling a wooden chariot. The vividly depicted harnessed terra cotta horses measure 1.5m in height and 2m in length. Most chariots have a single shaft measuring 3.7m in length and a diameter of between 8-16cm. The chariots measure 1.2m in length and 1.3m in width, with each of two wheels having 30 spokes. Five crossbeams form the frame of each chariot, with each having a railing and rear door measuring 60cm in width. The finely crafted chariots fully reflect the advanced craftsmanship of the period.

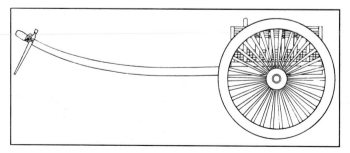

Blueprint of a restored chariot.

Remnants of chariot wheels.

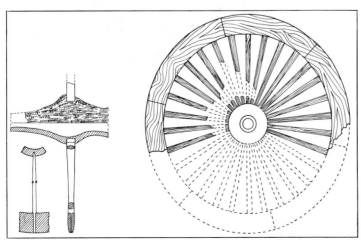

Blueprint of a restored chariot wheel.

Battle array in the No. 1 Trench.

Battle array in the No. 1 Trench.

Battle array in
the No. 1 Trench.

Battle array in the No. 1 Trench.

Vanguards in the No. 1 Trench viewed from the left.

Vanguards in the No. 1 Trench viewed from the right.

The left flank in the No. 1 Trench.

The right flank in the No. 1 Trench.

49

Exterior view of Exhibition Hall in the No. 2 Trench.

No. 2 Trench

The battle array in the No. 2 Trench is estimated to extend 124 meters from the east to the west and 98 meters from north to south. The trench is located some 20 meters east of the No. 1 Trench. Trial explorations and excavations indicate the trench may hold as many as 350 terra cotta chariot horses, 100 cavalry steeds, over 900 warriors from various ranks, and 89 wooden chariots. The array, shaped liked a carpenter's square, is composed of four small divisions which represent the powerful flank force protecting the main body in the No. 1 Trench.

The first small square formation occupies the first unit in the trench, and stretches into both the No. 2 Trench and area still further to the left. This particular arrangement greatly added to the battle efficiency of archers. The total formation of 230 crossbow archers, including 160 heavily armoured kneeling figurines in eight columns of 20 each. A number of other standing crossbow archers assume a shooting position to the rear. The battle array was highly effective when facing an enemy, with the two different shooting positions making it possible for archers to fire volleys at intervals in order to effectively stop the advancing enemy.

The second small square division situated to the right of the L-shaped formation is composed of 64 chariots divided into eight groups. The relatively new battle array introduced during the period has historically been referred to "light chariots". The former formation called the chariots to lead a squad of infantrymen. However, the new formation enabled the chariots to move faster and sustain their powerful charge. The new innovation indeed marked a periodic advancement in Chinese military history.

The third division in the center of square array consists of a combination of chariots, infantrymen and cavalrymen. The 19 chariots and support forces are divided into three columns, with six chariots in the first and third columns and seven in the second column. The figurine of a general is found in the last chariot in the third column. Another important change in this particular small square division centers on the fact the rear guard is composed of 32 infantrymen and eight cavalrymen, the first time the latter has been found in that position. Some theorized that the cavalrymen acted as messengers.

A fourth square cavalry division found the crossbow archers consists of chariots and 108 cavalrymen in column array. Each chariot holds two figurines, a charioteer and a scout. The nine ranks of cavalrymen are divided into three groups of four each. Each tall cavalryman with strong features wears full armor, and stands beside his mount holding a bow in one hand and reigns in the other. The muscular horses wearing saddles and blankets appear ready for immediate action.

The four small square divisions unite to form one larger unit referred to as a highly flexible "battle array within a battle array." The combination of chariots, infantrymen and cavalrymen represents a major change in battle arrays used after the Warring States Period. It also indicates the introduction of what "Strategist Sun Bin: the Eighth Battle Formation",

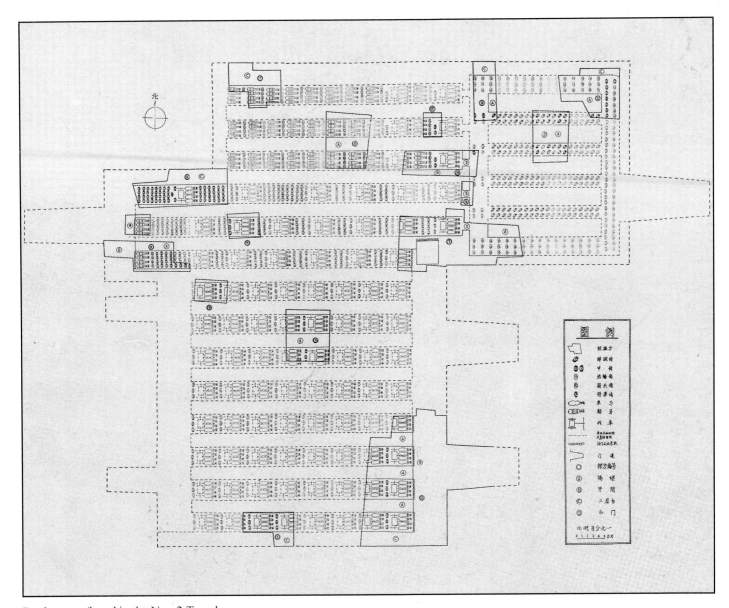

Battle array found in the No. 2 Trench.

describes as: "Chariots and cavalrymen divided into three
sections -- the right, left and rear. Chariots take the lead in
a smooth battle; the cavalry charges in dangerous situations;
and crossbow archers shower arrows on the enemy in critical
situations". The Qin army, in fact, employed Sun Bin's
strategy to defeat the State of Zhao.

Yuan Zhongyi, president of the Museum of Terra Cotta Warriors
and Horses, attends ground-breaking ceremony for the No. 2 Trench.

Excavated cavalrymen in the No. 2 Trench.

Excavated site in the No. 2 Trench.

The remnants of wood used to support the roof on the No. 2 Trench.

Excavated site in the No. 2 Trench.

Exterior view of Exhibition Hall of the No. 3 Trench.

No. 3 Trench

The battle array in the No. 3 Trench is situated 25 meters west of the north side of the No. 1 Trench and 120 meters east of the No. 2 Trench. The No. 3 Trench, which covers 500 square meters and is thus the smallest of the three trenches, has yielded 66 terra cotta figurines, four Chariot horses and one wooden chariot. Archeologists theorize that the trench represents the headquarters. No battle arrays are found in the trench, with figurines carrying bronze weapons facing each other while standing outside north and south rooms. The figurines are thought to be guarding the headquarters. The trench has also yielded animal bones and deer horns. Experts surmise the animals were offered as sacrifices prior to a battle.

The miniaturized buried Qin terra cotta army transports the vividness of the ancient imperial army in place over 2,200 years ago to contemporary times. It not only provides a view of the powerful military forces of Qin, but offers practical data concerning differing types of armed units, battle arrays, weapons distributions and strategic tactical thinking. The monumental discovery, which offers the opportunity to visualize many important historical battle arrays is quite appropriately referred to as a stereoscopic book on the art of war.

The No. 3 Trench.

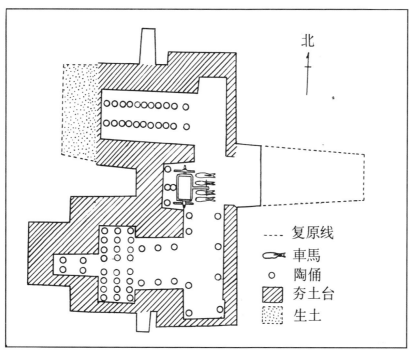

北

---- 复原线
车马
○ 陶俑
夯土台
生土

Battle array found in the No. 3 Trench.

Excavation in the northern
section of the No. 3 Trench.

Restored section of the No. 3 Trench.

Restored section of the No. 3 Trench.

Restored section of the No. 3 Trench.

Excavated corner of the No. 3 Trench.

Head of a painted terra cotta
warrior in the No. 3 Trench.

Head of a painted terra cotta
warrior in the No. 3 Trench.

Pieces of terra cotta warriors wearing painted armor in the No. 3 Trench.

III. Sculptures Reveal Great Artistic Attainment

Restored general.

The terra cotta figurines unearthed at the Qin Shi Huang Mausoleum represent a distinguished peak in the fruitful history of ancient Chinese sculpture, with their elegant demeanor truly representing a major chapter in the history of Oriental sculpture.

The numerous significant achievements of the Qin terra cotta figurines are readily discernible. However, the most significant achievement is perhaps the huge size and imposing manner of figurines representative of the powerful Qin army. The vast majority of awe-struck visitors leave the Qin Mausoleum overwhelmed by such a large number of terra cotta giants which form such a magnificent scene. The well over 7,000 terra cotta warriors and horses in full battle array spread over the more than 20,000 square meters appear to be prepared to confront the enemy at a moment's notice. Little imagination is required to visualize a massive swirling dust cloud which would blot out the sun and envelope the earth as they charged.

The height of the sculpted warriors averages around 1.8 meters, with some as tall as two meters. The horses are more realistically sized at 1.7 meters in height and 2 meters in length. While clay figurines dating to other historical periods have been unearthed in numerous other archeological digs, the Qin terra cotta figurines represent most significant find in terms of sheer numbers and size.

Yet another significant achievement rests with the realistic depictions of Qin terra cotta figurines. Some archeologists theorize that the differing features and expressions resulted from the fact that separate models posed for each figurine.

The accurately proportioned figurines vividly depict life as if they could breathe on their own. The same applies to muscular horses which stand with forelegs straight and hind legs slightly bent. The horses, with nostrils open wide, ears standing erect and eyes flaring, seemed to be ready to charge into battle at any moment.

The dress and facial expressions of Qin army figurines enables one to discern generals from the ranks of soldiers and warriors. For example, dignified and strongly built generals are adorned in double-layered robes covered by colored plate armor. They also wear brown caps and shoes curved upward. The long robes of soldiers are covered with armor, while their caps are taller and each is grasping a weapon. Their fearless look reveals countless life-and-death battle experience. Warriors, on the other hand, are depicted according to the branch of service for which they were trained. Some archers holding bows are depicted in a kneeling position with their right knee on the ground and left leg bent. Other archers are in a standing position with their left foot half a step in front of their right foot. In addition, they assume a shooting posture holding the bow in their extended left hand and arrow in the right hand close to their chest. They indeed appear ready to shower arrows on the enemy. The most impressive aspect of the figurines is perhaps the unique expressions on their faces. No two figurines have been found to have the exact same features, with some appearing to be frank and open men, while others appear to be solemn. Still others stare angrily ahead with knotted brow, some with tight lips and lowered eyes appear to be in deep thought, and others seem cheerful and naive.

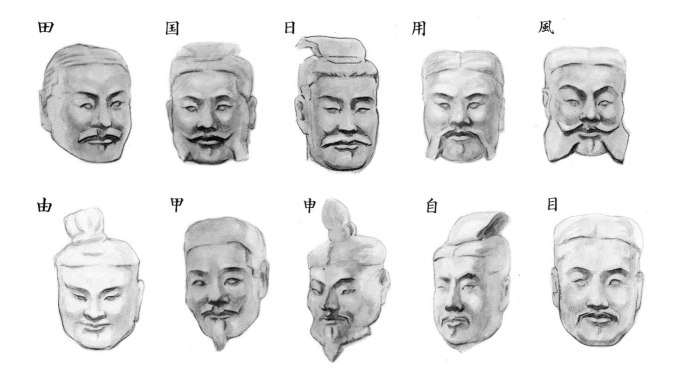

田　　　　国　　　　日　　　　用　　　　風

由　　　　甲　　　　申　　　　自　　　　目

Some archeologists suggest that facial features reveal the origins of the soldier. For example, one might have been a farmer from the Central Shaanxi plain, another a young man from Sichuan, and yet another a shepherd from the grasslands in northern China.

The coloring of Qin terra cotta figurines was another major achievement. Despite the peeling of brightly colored paint due to over 2,000 years of corrosion and a major fire, the flakes of remaining paint indicated the figurines were formerly covered with various bright colors such as red, green, blue, white, black and yellow. The imposing terra cotta figurines must have presented a magnificent scene prior to being buried in the trenches! The greatest level of effort and indeed the most monumental achievements can be found on the faces of the figurines. The long recognized fact that Qin Dynasty artists were highly skilled at depicting facial features was further verified by the Qin terra cotta figurines. Artists vividly depicted the foreheads, superciliary ridges, nose bridges, chins, cheeks and hair on all figurines. Various aspects such as superciliary ridges, lips, mustaches and ears were obviously exaggerated. However, the exaggerated parts perfectly matched other features and the faces appeared natural following the application of paint. The method revealed the perfect integration of coloring and sculpturing. Careful analyses have revealed that at least three layers of paint were applied to the faces of figurines. The first layer consisted of a brownish raw lacquer, with pink or a similar color added as the second layer, and a thin layer of white paint applied as the final touch. The technique truly brought out the shine and color of human skin. However, the greatest attention was paid to the eyes. The readily distinguishable black pupils in the yellowish brown irises of figurines reflected the fact that traditional Chinese sculpture and painting considered the eyes to the most important factor required to make a statue appear lifelike.

A combination of molding and sculpturing were employed to fashion the terra cotta figurines in the Qin Mausoleum. Traditional sculpturing methods used included layering, pinching, pasting, carving and painting. Long strips of clay were layered to form the rough outline of the body, with the pasting, pinching and carving methods employed to add robes and armor. Fashioning heads represented a comparatively complicated process. Facial features were achieved using a mold, with piling and sculpting used to form the back of the head. Ears were pasted to the heads prior to adding sculpted or molded hair buns. Refinements such as eyes, eyebrows, mouths, mustaches and ears were carefully carved to reveal the desired personality for the figurine.

Examinations of the Qin terra cotta figurines also revealed the excellence of clay figurine firing techniques. Analyses of broken pieces revealed that the figurines were baked at temperatures ranging between 950-1059 degrees Celsius. The pure luster, high density and hardness level of clay in most figurines is readily apparent. Modern attempts to duplicate the ancient baking process have, in fact, failed to produce figurines of equal quality.

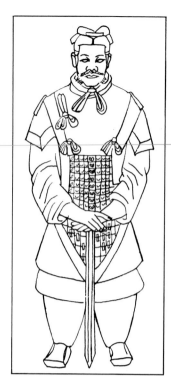

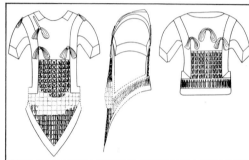

Armorclad general with a sword unearthed in the No. 1 Trench: This particular figurine, standing some 197cm in height, is wearing two layers of robes covered by a small armor cape covering his shoulders, and shin guards protecting his legs. His square-toed shoes curve upwards and he is wearing brown headgear. The general's arms are crossed, with his hands appearing to be resting on the handles of a sword.

Armor: This particular kind of armor designed for generals protects the chest, back and shoulders. The front section of the armor cape, which is 96.5cm in length, covers the chest and abdomen, with the 61cm long rear section covering the back and waist. Some 160 pieces of 4cm square bronze pieces were used to fashion the cape. The shoulders and edges of the armor cape are decorated with geometrical patterns, with eight flowers made of ribbon used to decorate the front plate, three flower patterns the back plate and one flower each for the upper arm plate.

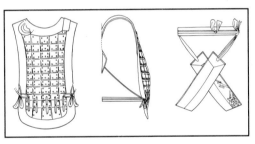

Junior officer unearthed in No. 2 Trench: This junior officer is wearing trousers and a high-collar shirt under an armor cape. His square-toed shoes curve upwards and he is wearing a flat bun on his head. The specialty armor, which covers the chest but not the back or shoulders, was fashioned from a piece of leather inlaid with pieces of bronze in various shapes. The eight lines on the chest include 11 pieces of bronze each, with three lines on the lower section including five pieces of bronze each. The leather is inlaid with square, rectangular and irregularly shaped pieces of bronze.

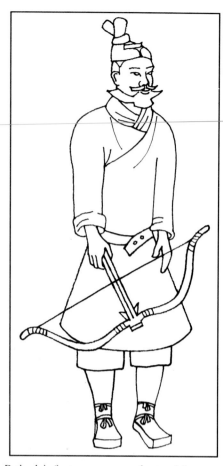

Robed infantryman, or foot soldier, unearthed at the east end of No. 1 Trench. The
soldier is wearing a knee-length robe, short
trousers and a belt. Pieces of cloth are wrapped
tightly around his own legs and his shoes curve
slightly towards the ankles. The soldier wears
a bun on the top of his head, but no helmet.
The fact that he wears no armor allows for un-
restricted movement.

Light infantry archer unearthed in No. 1 Trench. The archer, some 186cm in height, stands erect wearing a long red robe and belt. He also wears short green trousers and white shin guards to protect his legs, as well as a pair of low-cut red boots. The archer, with a bun on the top of his head, assumes a posture with one foot half a step in front of the other. His body is turned slightly to the left, with his left arm raised and right arm in front of his chest as if ready to shoot at any time.

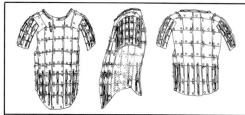

Armorclad infantryman: Armorclad infantrymen unearthed in No. 3 Trench, between 182-186cm in height, wear robes covered by turtleneck armor capes. They also wear short trousers, shin guards and curve-toed shoes. Each, which has a bun arranged slightly to one side of their heads, holds a wood or bamboo weapon portrayed with bronze.

Armor: A substantial number of the figures wear turtleneck armor capes designed to protect the chest, back and shoulders. Chest plates measure 62cm in length, back plates 58cm and shoulder plates 20.8cm. Eight lines of bronze pieces lines the chest plate, seven lines the back plate and four lines the shoulder plate. The lines are made of between 5 to 7 pieces of bronze.

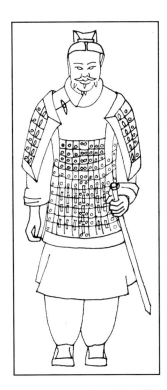

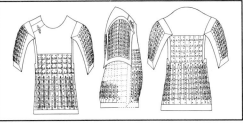

Lower echelon soldier unearthed in No. 1 Trench: The figurine, some 189cm in height, assumes a posture leaning slightly forward and appears to have been holding a sword in his left hand. His right hand is also clenched into a half fist as if he were holding something. He wears a red cap and green shin guards. His armor cape is made of dark brown pieces of bronze linked by red string.

Armor: Three of the lower echelon soldiers unearthed are wearing armor capes of the aforementioned style. The armor consists of a front, back and shoulder plates, with both the front and back plates measuring some 64cm in length. The armor cape was fashioned from leather inlaid with pieces of bronze, with both the front and back plates having 11 lines of inlaid bronze pieces.

War chariot unearthed in No. 2 Trench: This open single-shaft two-wheeled chariot was pulled by a team of four horses and was manned by a squad of three soldiers standing in a single line, with two soldiers flanking the charioteer in the center. The charioteer wears a long robe under an armor cape which covers his chest, back and shoulders. The shoulder section of the cape drops to the armpits, with his hands protected by reinforced gloves and legs by shin guards. He also wears a helmet which covers the back portion of the neck. The charioteer's arms are extended as if he were holding the reins. The accompanying soldiers wear long robes covered by armor capes, with shin guards protecting their legs. Both soldiers wear buns with headpieces, and carry long weapons in one hand while grasping the chariot with the other.

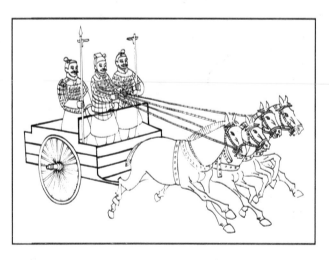

Staff officer (general) unearthed in the No. 2 Trench. The general wears colored armor which resembles fish scales, and a brown cap. The armor has no shoulder covers, but instead covers only his chest and back. The front cover, with a pointed edge, is 100.8cm in length. The edges of the armor sections are decorated with colored patterns some 6cm in width.

Front-rank soldier unearthed in the No.1 Trench: This figurine, some 191cm in height, wears a knee-length robe covered by an armor cape with shoulder covers. He wears a pair of short trousers, with strips of cloth wrapped tightly around his lower legs. He also wears a tall helmet and simply designed shoes. He was obviously holding a long weapon in his right hand, and appears to have been holding an as yet undetermined object in his left hand.

Kneeling archers found in No. 2 Trench. The 160-odd kneeling archers kneel on their right knees in the middle of a large unit. The figurines are 120cm in height. Their arms are extended in front of their chests in a shooting position. Some scholars suggest that the archers knelt on one leg to cock the crossbow and then stood erect before firing.

Frontal view of kneeling archer.

Rear view of kneeling archer.

Full-body view of kneeling archer.

Sole of an archer's boot.

Terra cotta warriors in the No. 1 Trench.

Head of a light infantryman in the No. 1 Trench.

Head of an armorclad soldier in the No. 1 Trench.

Head of a charioteer in the No. 1 Trench.

Head of light infantryman in the No. 1 Trench.

Head of a light infantryman in the No. 1 Trench.

  Facial characteristics of terra cotta warriors: Facial features were added to molded heads by employing techniques such as piling, pasting, pinching, carving and painting.   Each figurine had unique facial characteristics, with no two terra cotta soldiers unearthed thus far having the same features.   The craftsmanship involved in fashioning the figurines was heavily influenced by traditional Chinese sculpture which integrated area and stressed lines.   Protruding parts of the faces exhibited are sharply carved, with heavy paint applied to minimize the sharpness. Traditional techniques, including sculpting, painting and drawn lines, were used to depict facial features, hair, ears and mustaches.

79

Hairstyles of terra cotta warriors: The hairstyles of terra cotta warriors soldiers have been divided into three groups. The first style involved parting hair in the middle of the head and then braiding same with hair above the ears. The hair on the back of the head was also braided and then integrated with hair on one side of the head to form a bun. The second style involved forming a bun on the top of the head, followed by making six braids which were then pinned tightly to the back of the head. The final style involved fashioning a bun on top of the head, followed by adding a tiny cap with a ribbon which could be tied under the chin. The third style also featured six braids pinned to the back of the head.

Paint fragments on the head of a terra cotta warrior.

Paint fragments on the head of a terra cotta warrior.

Paint fragments on the head of a terra cotta warrior.

Paint fragments on the head of a terra cotta warrior.

Paint fragments on the head of a terra cotta warrior.

Paint fragments on the head of a terra cotta warrior.

Paint fragments on the head of a terra cotta warrior.

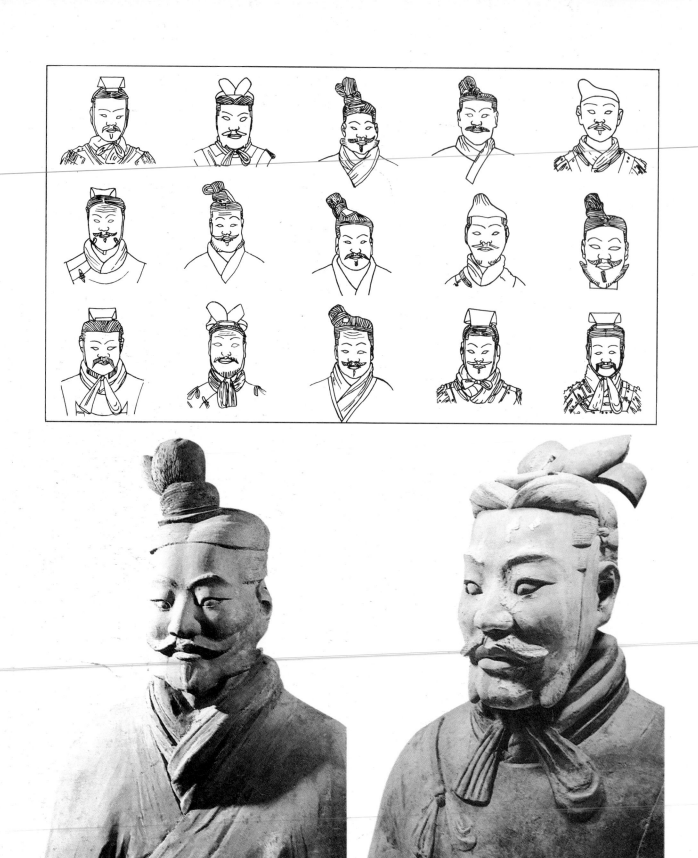

Beards and mustaches on terra cotta warriors: Ancient Chinese believed that facial hair was sacred and should be saved. The vast majority of terra cotta warriors thus adorn beards or mustaches in seven styles as shown here.

No. 1 Trench.

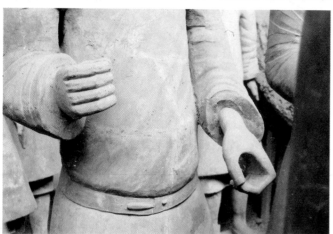

Hand positions of terra cotta warriors: The hands of terra cotta warriors are depicted in various positions. Some feature bare hands dangling alongside the body, with others grasping swords or reining a horse, and still others holding long weapons.

Belt buckles: The extensive variety of buckles on belts worn by terra cotta warriors reflected the colorful life in the Qin Dynasty. The numerous shapes included spades, axes and musical instruments, with some featuring object in relief. One interesting buckle features a relief depiction of a warrior leaning forward and clutching a spear in his hand. The tongue on this particular buckle was fashioned to look like the head of an enemy.

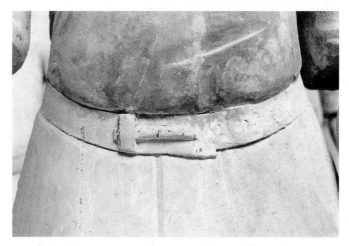

Shoes and boots: The terra cotta warriors feature boots and
four particular types of shoes and boots: boots, shoes with
curved tops, tilted shoes, pointed tops and plain tops.

Inscriptions: Carved or printed inscriptions featuring the names of craftsmen have been found on many terra cotta warriors. Most inscriptions are found on the backs of robes, while others are found on the arms, legs and armor. The names of over 80 craftsmen have thus far been discovered on the figurines.

Chariot squad member: This particular figurine, some 193.5cm in height, wears a green blouse under a dark brown armor cape. The cape protects his upper body, with shin guards protecting his legs. His outstretched right arm indicates that he was holding a weapon with a long handle, and he appears to have been clutching a sword in his left hand. The handsome square-jawed warrior exhibits an air of solemnity.

Section of the No. 1 Trench.

Charioteer unearthed in the No. 1 Trench: The charioteer wears a tall narrow cap and armor cape. His duties included was to drive his war chariot and assume command if the commander was wounded.

Profile of charioteer.

Profile of charioteer.

Rear view of charioteer.

Head of an archer.

Hairstyle of an armorclad warrior.

Infantryman: This figurine wearing a blouse and leather belt
stands 187.5cm in height.   He wears knee-length trousers,   with
strips of cloth wrapped tightly around his lower legs.   He adorns
a tall narrow cap and a pair of shoes with tilted tops.   He appears
to be holding a long-handled weapon in his raised right hand.

Painted head of an armorclad warrior.

Armorclad warrior.

Armorclad warrior.

Head of an armorless soldier unearthed in the No. 1 Trench.

Infantrymen found in the No. 1 Trench.

Armorclad warrior.

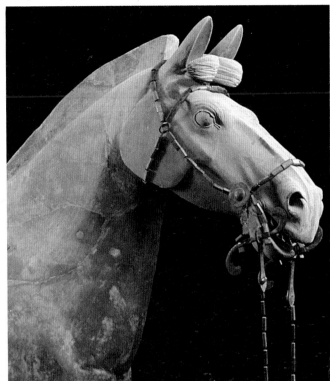

Head of a battle horse.

Mounted cavalrymen: This particular figurine was unearthed in No. 2 Trench. The warrior, some 180cm in height, wears a narrow-sleeved knee-length blouse and belt under an armor cape. He wears long narrow trousers and boots, as well as a round cap. The warrior holds the reins in one hand and a crossbow in the other.

The saddle, which appears to have been made of leather, is secured to the horse with a single girth.

Horse's head.

Terra cotta horses: More than 600 horses have been excavated from the No. 1, No. 2 and No. 3 trenches. Two kinds of horses have been found—battle steeds and chariot teams. The four-horse chariot teams are closer to the actual size, with each measuring some 2 meters in length and 1.72 meters in height. The chariot teams feature strong limbs, large head, protruding noses, short necks and wide shoulders. The muscular horses appear ready for action with ears erect and flaring eyes. Some with raised heads and open mouths appearing to be neighing.

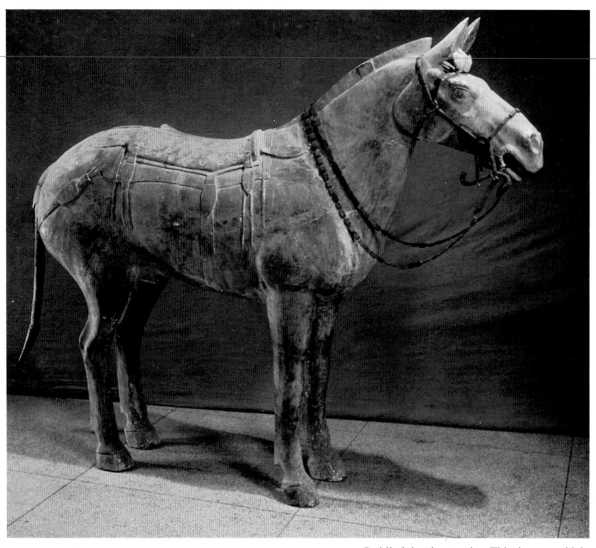

Saddled battle steed: This horse, which stands 172cm in height and is 203cm in length, has short mane and a neatly combed tail. The red, white, brown and blue saddle sits atop a green blanket. The saddle is secured to the horse's back with a single girth.

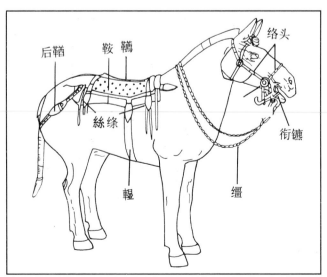

后鞧　　鞍韂　　　　　　络头

絲绦

鞦　　　　彊　　衔镳

Saddled horse.

Terra cotta horse.

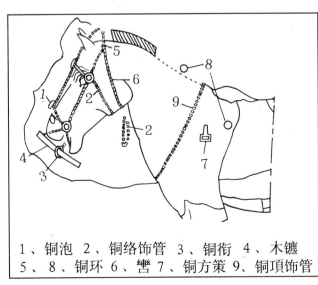

1、铜泡 2、铜络饰管 3、铜衔 4、木镳
5、8、铜环 6、𫛜 7、铜方策 9、铜項饰管

Head of a terra cotta horse.

Bridle

Terra cotta soldiers and chariots in the No. 1 Trench form an eastwardly facing rectangular battle array measuring 184x57 meters. The infantry, with weapons in hand, stand ready for battle. The battle array is armed with an extensive variety of weapons, with archers at the front and soldiers with long-handled weapons to the rear. The arrangement of light and heavy weapons gives full play to the army's advantages. Charioteers grasping reins are also prepared for action.

IV. Exquisite Weaponry of the Qin Army

Wood and bamboo weapons.

The designers of the Qin Mausoleum extended the greatest possible effort to ensure that the terra cotta warriors closely replicated members of the emperor's army. Each figurine was, in fact, armed with a bronze weapon -- the preferred weaponry of the period. Well over 10,000 bronze weapons have already been unearthed in the mere 10 percent of the burial site thus far excavated. The extensive array of armaments, which include almost every type of weapon used by the Qin army, includes dozens of varieties of swords, daggers, battle-axes, halberds, double-bladed spears, bows and arrows and swords with curved blades, as well as numerous wood and bamboo weapons.

Most of the unearthed weaponry was designed for distance fighting, with 130 sites at the east end of the No. 1 Trench alone yielding 279 arrows and 10,896 arrowheads, as well as 22 bronze swords. Each of the excavated swords measured some 90cm in length. The shine and sharp blades on the weapons serve as a ready reminder of famous Tang Dynasty Poet Li Bai's poem describing Qin swords: "The blue sky reflects the shine of the swords. "

Archeologists were quite surprised to discover 31 wood and bamboo weapons, which they later surmised had been carried by honor guards. The most significant discovery, however, was double-bladed spears known as "Pi. " The heads of the never before seen ancient weapons are shaped like a sword. However, the blades are sharp and the shafts are longer than those used for spears. The discovery of the unique weapons corrected the historical misconception that "Pi"

were short swords. A majority of the weapons feature long shafts, with the longest measuring 3.82 meters. "Pi" have the longest shafts, followed by halberds. The wood or bamboo shafts were tightly wound with thread, lacquered and decorated with red lines. While many weapons bear carved inscriptions, the greatest number can be found on battle-axes and "Pi." The inscriptions record the names of manufacturers, officials monitoring the manufacturing process and individual weaponsmith. The inscriptions are invaluable records for research into the development of Chinese weaponry, the management system for weapons manufacturing, and the evolution of ancient Chinese written characters.

The weapons were cast, finely ground, sanded and processed by as yet undetermined techniques. The process yielded weapons with a refined appearance and sharp blades. The various shapes of Qin swords revealed the extensive development of the processing method. The high-level accuracy of the finely ground blades and bridges of swords equals modern pieces processed by machine. The triangular or pyramidal arrowheads were crafted with incredible accuracy. The surface of arrowheads featured the sectional curvature of a bullet, with the accuracy of the three tines on triangular arrowheads shown to match almost perfectly at 20: 1 magnification. Error factors were, in fact, found to be 0.15mm or less.

Weapons were finely coated with a 10 micron layer of rustproof chromic salt oxide -- a technique which defied development in Europe and America until contemporary times.

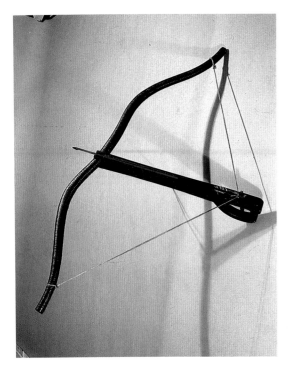

Crossbow.

Arrows and arrowheads.

Crossbow trigger.

Despite having been buried for more than 2,000 years, the sharpness of the swords was readily apparent following removal of the rustproof coating. An irregular cloud-shaped pattern on the surface of the shinning bronze double-bladed spears suggested a unique processing technique. While scientists have determined the pattern was neither the result of casting or carving, the actual cause remains unknown. However, some scholars suggest that the pattern was the result of vulcanization.

Qin weapons contain significantly more tin than those dating to the earlier Yin and Zhou dynasties. The copper content in bronze swords found in the Qin Mausoleum was 71-74.6 percent, with the level of tin standing at 21.38-31 percent. Spears, on the other hand, contained 69.62 percent copper and 30.38 percent tin. The copper and tin content in bronze weapons closely matches figures found in the work entitled " Artificers Records. " Reasonable levels of different metals have also been found in other weapons. The aforementioned facts provide ample proof of the high-level skill of weaponsmiths in the Qin Dynasty.

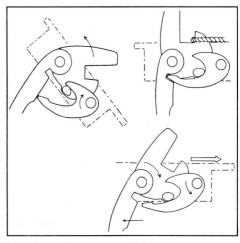

Crossbow trigger assembly.

Battle-axe.

Spear.

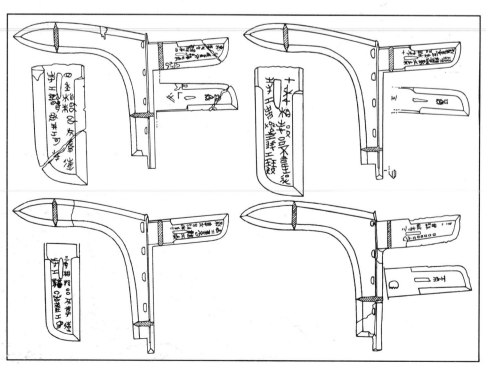

Battle-axes.

Double-blade spear.

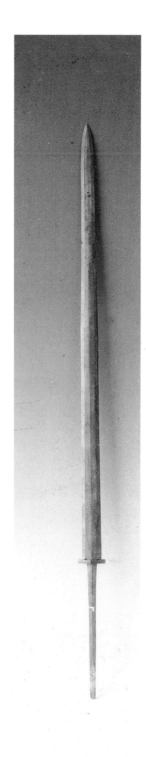

Double-blade spear.

Curved sword.

V.   The Splendid Imperial Carriages of Emperor Qin Shi Huang

The glorious magnificence of ancient imperial carriages is undeniable. While historians from many dynasties offered lengthy descriptions of magnificent and luxurious imperial carriages, no actual examples were unearthed until the 1980s when archeologists discovered a 55x55 meter trench yielding a number of bronze carriages. The replications provided people with their first ever glimpse of the imperial carriages of Emperor Qin Shi Huang.

Both of the carriage units initially unearthed included a coachman and harnessed four horse team. The burial site in question covered 3,025 square meters located some 20 meters west of the Qin Mausoleum. In addition, 10 bronze carriages in five separate groups were detected in five smaller trenches in Section II.

The initial excavation of the burial site in 1980 yielded two large brightly painted imperial carriages. Both single-shaft carriages had two wheels, and unit included a team of four bronze horses and a coachman. The length of the bronze carriage units, including teams of horses, measured 2.25m and 3.17m respectively, with each standing approximately one meter in height, or about half of the true size. The cache of carriages consisted of more than 6,000 parts, including items as large of bronze horses weighing over 200 kilograms each, and tiny decorative adornments weighing less than 50 grams. The excellent craftsmanship on the carriage units featured the vivid facial expression of coachmen and exquisite intact linkages between finer parts. The carriage units are truly unprecedented masterpieces in the history of bronze casting, with Professor Su Bai, a famous archeologist, referring to them as "the ultimate in bronze objects. "

Each unit included a carriage, coachman and four horse team. The rectangular car of the lead carriage, often referred to as the "inspection carriage, " measured 48.5cm in length and 74cm in width. The front and sides of the carriage were enclosed, with the rear remaining open for convenient ingress or egress. The imperial coachman standing at the front, with outstretched arms holding the reins, was shielded from the sun by an umbrella. In addition, the carriage featured finely cast bronze weapons such as bows, arrows and shields.

The rear carriage, often referred to as the "rest carriage, " was divided into two sections, with the coachman reigning the team of horses from the front section. The spacious enclosed rear section,   measuring 80x78cm, was the domain of the emperor. The emperor's was readily distinguishable because of its arched roof and door.

Primary research strongly suggests that the 10 carriages found in the trench were exact duplicates of carriage units used by Emperor Qin Shi Huang, with the trench itself replicating the imperial carriage house. Nonetheless, the concentrated grandeur of the discovery represented nothing more than a tiny segment of the numerous fleet of carriages used by the first emperor in Chinese history. The so-called "carriage team system" was devised to fulfill political requirements for the emperor to conduct inspection tours of his vast territory. The system called for three different sizes of carriage teams, with more important tours requiring 81 carriages, less important tours 36 units, and normal tours only nine units. Archeologists suggest that the carriages discovered in the initial dig were used for normal tours. The discovery yielded five "inspection" and an equal number of "rest" carriages.

The unearthed carriages are currently exhibited in the Museum of Qin Terra Cotta Warriors and Horses. When viewing the brilliance of the brightly colored imperial wagons, one cannot help but visualize the magnificent scene of an imperial tour. There is little wonder why Liu Bang, who as a youngster witnessed an imperial tour by Qin Shi Huang and himself became emperor after overthrowing the Qin Dynasty, sighed in admiration and commented: "This is indeed the way a true man should live!"

Although only half their true size, the high-level realism of the replicated imperial carriages is readily apparent due to the strictly proportioned carriages and horses which are accurately depicted to the most minute detail. Said realism not only applies to their respective shapes, but also to their overall appearance. For example, the true texture of bronze leather mats, ropes, the mane and tails of horses and the fabric on wagons is readily discernible. The discovery of the imperial carriages and terra cotta figurines representing the Qin army created a revolution in the understanding of ancient Chinese sculpture.

The vivid depictions of coachmen are central to the exquisite molding techniques of the Qin Dynasty, and indeed to the overall development of molding in ancient China. The bronze figurines were not only precisely molded, but were also vividly exhibited. The presentation accurately

The restored No. 1 (front) and No. 2 carriages.

reveals the high esteem of emperor, while at the same time revealing the prudent and humble look on the faces of coachmen. Nonetheless, their seeming complacency is betrayed by the proud looks in their eyes and the slight scours apparent on their lips. The ribbons on their official robes, the brown caps on their heads and the swords in their waistbands reveal their rank. Their facial expressions echoed the mastery of horsemanship revealed in the way they hold the reins. The equally lifelike depictions of harnessed horses are also readily apparent. The stately alert steeds, with protruding muscles, erect ears, flaring eyes and raised head, appear ready to gallop away at any moment.

The bodies and wheels of carriages are heavily decorated, with each carriage featuring some 2,000 gold and silver ornaments. For example, the high-rank of the owner of No. 2 carriage is revealed by eye-catching adornments on the carriage and horses which are decorated with 737 pieces of gold and 983 pieces of silver.

The bronze carriages were originally painted with bright rich colors ranging from vermilion, pink, green, fresh green, emerald green, cobalt blue and sky blue to white, black and brown. The craftsmen cleverly achieved harmony despite dealing with complicated structures and rich colors. The good taste apparent in the use of bright colors is yet another aspect revealing the profound artistic attainment and excellent coloring skills of the Qin craftsmen.

More than ten varieties of patterns were used to mold over 100 sections of the carriages. The most frequently used patterns depicted dragons, phoenixes, diamonds, clouds and geometric designs. The rational arrangement of the patterns, which in some sections were neatly piled and in other's barely visible, suggested a typical painting style in ancient China.

The excavation of imperial carriages: Two bronze carriages were unearthed to the west of the Qin Mausoleum in 1980. Both single-shaft carriages, some 2.5 meters in length, were facing west. The colorful square carriages are decorated with geometric and cloud-shaped patterns.

Standing on the front carriage is the coachman armed with a sword, while the kneeling coachman on the rear carriage is wearing double-tailed cap and long blouse. The four horse teams pulling carriages have flowing patterns on their bodies. Each harnessed horse measures

72cm in height and 120cm in length. The bodies of the horses are decorated with gold and silver ornaments. The excavation site shown here includes both the No. 1 and No. 2 carriages.

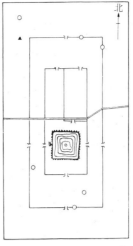

Excavation site of bronze carriages.

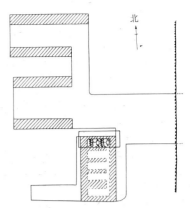

Burial site of bronze carriages.

The carriages rank as the most representative work revealing Qin Dynasty attainments in metal smelting, molding, processing and assembling. Assembling the carriages, which are imposing in terms of size, required exquisite skill at using an extensive variety of parts. In fact, assembling many of the parts with either curves of corners is considered to be a demanding job even today. The arched roof on No. 2 Carriage, which was molded in one piece, covers 2.3 square meters, but has a thickness ranging between a mere 1-4 mm. The absence of excellent casting techniques would have made it impossible to mold such a large arched piece with only a minimal thickness. Qin Dynasty craftsmen did an excellent job even in terms of modern standards. The metal processing and assembly techniques used to craft the carriages are equally impressive. The assembly process required over 7,500 links and 1,000 welds to connect well over 7,000 parts. The excellent work required to accomplish such exquisite and complicated carriages truly reveal the outstanding attainments of the Qin Dynasty craftsmen. Their accomplishment indeed represent a glorious page in the history of metal processing in China and the world as a whole.

The No. 2 Carriage shortly after excavation.

Restoration of the No. 1 Carriage roof.

Broken wheel from the No. 1 Carriage.

Restorers repair the No. 1 Carriage.

The No. 1 Carriage.

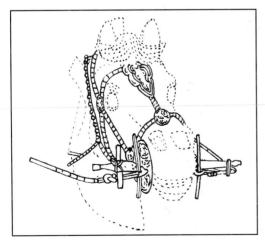

Bridle (left side).

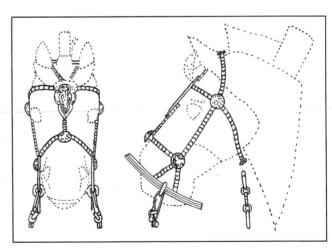

Bridle (right side).

The No. 2 Carriage.

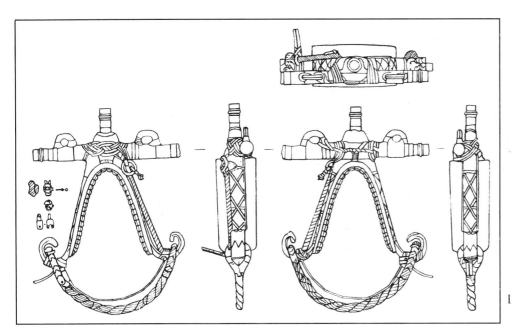

Left yoke.

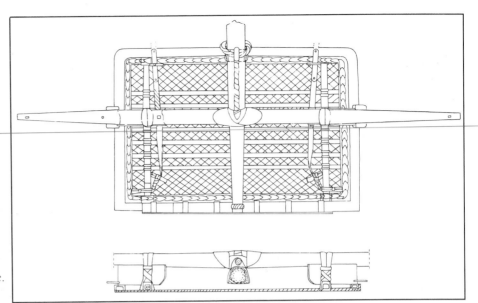

Frame of the No. 1 Carriage.

Section of the No. 1 Carriage.

Section of the No. 2 Carriage.

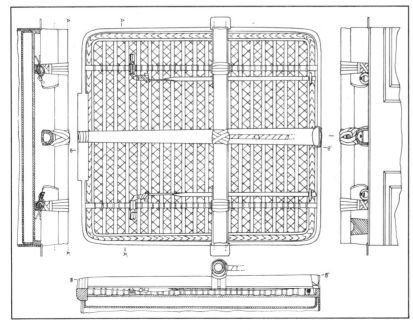

Frame of the No. 2 Carriage: Preventing carriages from overturning required the equal distribution of weights on the shafts.

Profile of the front section of the No. 1 Carriage.

Inner front section of the No. 1 Carriage.

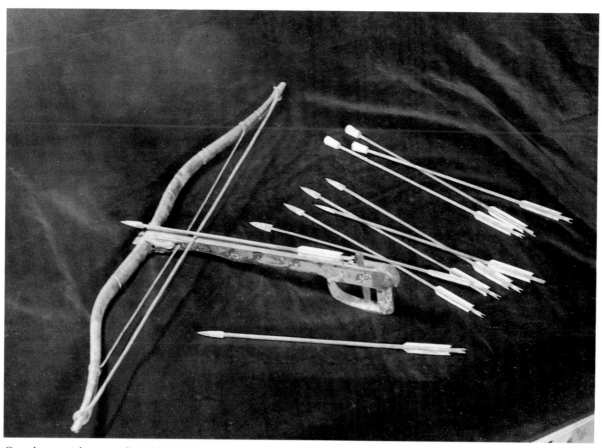

Crossbows and arrows found in carriages.

The arrows and quivers found in carriages.

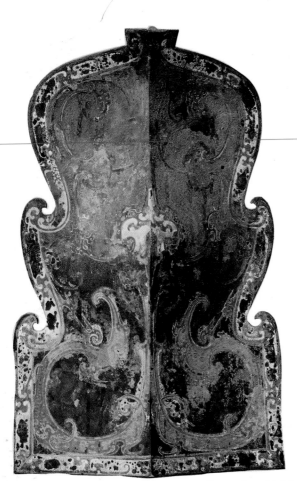

Protective shield on the No. 2 Carriage.

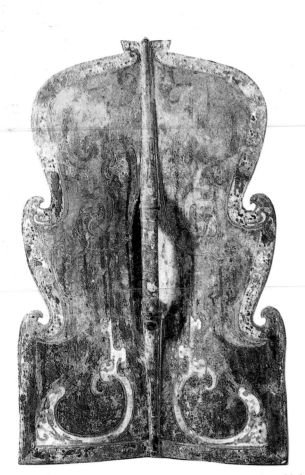
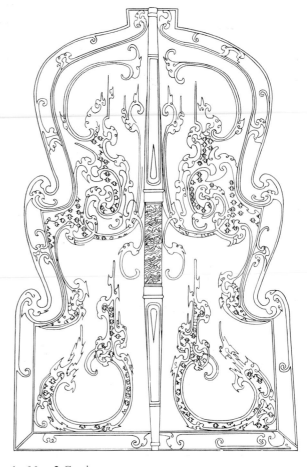

Rear protective shield on the No. 2 Carriage.

Interior patterns decorating door of the No. 2 Carriage.

顾　　问：秦始皇兵馬俑博物馆馆長　袁仲一

主　　编：秦始皇兵馬俑博物馆副馆長　考古隊隊長　張仲立

副 主 编：刘晓花　宋江安　覃仕英

责任编辑：袁天才

摄　　形：夏居宪　張国柱　高玉英　罗忠民　杨异同　童　辉

绘　　图：童辉

版式设计：袁天才　宋江安

封面设计：吴寿松

翻译 (英)：张凤茹　刘小红　罗伯特·比特

秦始皇陵兵馬俑

秦始皇兵馬俑博物馆考古隊编

*

人民中国出版社出版

（中国北京车公庄大街 3 号）

邮政编碼: 100044

外文印刷厂印刷

西安新城旅游图书发行社发行

889×1194　1/16　8 印张　30 千字

1997 年 4 月（英）第一版

ISBN7-80065-590-3/J · 090（外）

0010000